ARIES

ELEMENT:
Fire

MODALITY:
Cardinal

PLANETARY RULER:
Mars

ASTROLOGICAL OPPOSITE:
Libra

The Ram
March 21–April 19

AT THEIR BEST:
Courageous, enthusiastic, independent, bold, ambitious

AT THEIR WORST:
Willful, aggressive, selfish, impulsive, childlike

Famous Aries

Maya Angelou · Alec Baldwin · Ram Dass · Lady Gaga
Hugh Hefner · Elton John · Lil Nas X · Nancy Pelosi
Diana Ross · Reese Witherspoon

TAURUS

ELEMENT:
Earth

MODALITY:
Fixed

PLANETARY
RULER:
Venus

ASTROLOGICAL
OPPOSITE:
Scorpio

The Bull
April 20–May 20

AT THEIR BEST:
Dependable, patient,
resourceful, generous,
compassionate

AT THEIR WORST:
Rigid, vain, indulgent,
possessive, insecure

Famous Taurus

Aidy Bryant • John Cena • Cher • Tina Fey • Gigi Hadid
Janet Jackson • Dwayne "The Rock" Johnson
Grace Jones • Lizzo • Sam Smith

GEMINI

ELEMENT:
Air

MODALITY:
Mutable

PLANETARY RULER:
Mercury

ASTROLOGICAL OPPOSITE:
Sagittarius

The Twins
May 21–June 20

AT THEIR BEST:
Communicative, curious, witty, charming, intelligent

AT THEIR WORST:
Restless, manipulative, nervous, unreliable, gossipy

Famous Gemini

Naomi Campbell • James Charles • Bob Dylan • Prince
John F. Kennedy • Kanye West • Marilyn Monroe
Kendrick Lamar • Stevie Nicks • Mary-Kate and Ashley Olsen

CANCER

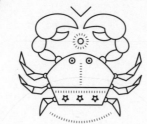

ELEMENT:
Water

MODALITY:
Cardinal

PLANETARY RULER:
Moon

ASTROLOGICAL OPPOSITE:
Capricorn

The Crab
June 21–July 22

AT THEIR BEST:
Sensitive, nurturing,
imaginative, perceptive,
supportive

AT THEIR WORST:
Moody, suspicious,
smothering, insecure,
closed off

Famous Cancer

Anthony Bourdain · Larry David · Lana del Rey
Elizabeth Gilbert · Ariana Grande · Kevin Hart · Post Malone
Meryl Streep · Robin Williams · Malala Yousafzai

LEO

ELEMENT:
Fire

MODALITY:
Fixed

PLANETARY RULER:
Sun

ASTROLOGICAL OPPOSITE:
Aquarius

The Lion
July 23–August 22

AT THEIR BEST:
Creative, enthusiastic, playful, funny, affectionate

AT THEIR WORST:
Dramatic, codependent, arrogant, self-absorbed, domineering

Famous Leo

James Baldwin · Coolio · Mick Jagger · Kylie Jenner
Dan Levy · Jennifer Lopez · Madonna · Barack Obama
Maya Rudolph · Martha Stewart

VIRGO

ELEMENT:
Earth

MODALITY:
Mutable

PLANETARY RULER:
Mercury

ASTROLOGICAL OPPOSITE:
Pisces

The Maiden
August 23–September 22

AT THEIR BEST:
Thoughtful, hardworking, loyal, sensitive, practical

AT THEIR WORST:
Rigid, worrying, judgmental, overly critical, righteous

Famous Virgo

Chimamanda Ngozi Adichie • Beyoncé • Leonard Cohen
Blake Lively • Freddie Mercury • Bill Murray • Mother Teresa
Bernie Sanders • Amy Winehouse • Zendaya

MIND PROGRESS CHANGE

VIRGO

LET'S GROW TOGETHER

TRUST
+ THE +
PROCESS

IT'S OK
YOU'RE
ONLY
HUMAN

VOL 10 THINGS I OVER-THOUGHT

VIRGO

♍

You Got This

LIBRA

ELEMENT:
Air

MODALITY:
Cardinal

PLANETARY RULER:
Venus

ASTROLOGICAL OPPOSITE:
Aries

The Scales
September 23–October 22

AT THEIR BEST:
Intellectual, charming, romantic, balanced, adaptable

AT THEIR WORST:
Dishonest, indecisive, avoidant, people-pleasing, neurotic

Famous Libra

Cardi B • Ta-Nehisi Coates • Snoop Dogg • Kamala Harris
Kim Kardashian West • Marie Kondo • Gwyneth Paltrow
Alexandria Ocasio-Cortez • Bruce Springsteen • Serena Williams

SCORPIO

ELEMENT:
Water

MODALITY:
Fixed

PLANETARY RULER:
Mars

ASTROLOGICAL OPPOSITE:
Taurus

The Scorpion
October 23–November 21

AT THEIR BEST:
Intense, mysterious, intuitive, passionate, investigative

AT THEIR WORST:
Explosive, vengeful, obsessive, possessive, destructive

Famous Scorpio

Joe Biden · Björk · Drake · Bill Gates · Joni Mitchell
Frank Ocean · Pablo Picasso · Sylvia Plath
Tracee Ellis Ross · Winona Ryder

ENJOY YOUR TIME ALIVE

SAGITTARIUS

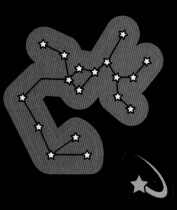

LIFE IS AN ADVENTURE

SAGITTARIUS

FREE SPIRIT

SHINE BRIGHT

WHERE YOUR FOCUS GOES YOUR ENERGY SHALL FLOW

SAGITTARIUS

✦

ELEMENT:
Fire

MODALITY:
Mutable

PLANETARY
RULER:
Jupiter

ASTROLOGICAL
OPPOSITE:
Gemini

✦

The Archer
November 22–December 21

AT THEIR BEST:
Adventurous, spontaneous,
idealistic, wise, honest

AT THEIR WORST:
Impatient, fanatic, restless,
confrontational, frank

Famous Sagittarius

Shirley Chisholm • Walt Disney • Billie Eilish • Jay-Z
Nicki Minaj • Jim Morrison • Brad Pitt • Britney Spears
Taylor Swift • Chrissy Teigen

CAPRICORN

ELEMENT:
Earth

MODALITY:
Cardinal

PLANETARY RULER:
Saturn

ASTROLOGICAL OPPOSITE:
Cancer

The Sea Goat
December 22–January 19

AT THEIR BEST:
Ambitious, grounded,
distinguished, disciplined,
dependable

AT THEIR WORST:
Materialistic, stubborn,
controlling, opportunistic,
overly guarded

Famous Capricorn

David Bowie • Timothée Chalamet • Janis Joplin
Martin Luther King Jr. • Richard Nixon • Lin-Manuel Miranda
Michelle Obama • Dolly Parton • Shonda Rhimes • Patti Smith

AQUARIUS

ELEMENT:
Air

MODALITY:
Fixed

**PLANETARY
RULER:**
Saturn

**ASTROLOGICAL
OPPOSITE:**
Leo

The Water Bearer
January 20–February 18

AT THEIR BEST:
Rebellious, insightful,
self-assured, original,
progressive

AT THEIR WORST:
Aloof, unpredictable,
stubborn, shocking,
detached

Famous Aquarius

Angela Davis • James Dean • Ellen DeGeneres
Guy Fieri • Toni Morrison • Yoko Ono • Ed Sheeran
Megan Thee Stallion • Harry Styles • Oprah Winfrey

PISCES

ELEMENT:
Water

MODALITY:
Mutable

PLANETARY RULER:
Jupiter

ASTROLOGICAL OPPOSITE:
Virgo

The Fish
February 19–March 20

AT THEIR BEST:
Intuitive, creative, sensitive, compassionate, spiritual

AT THEIR WORST:
Self-indulgent, spacey, avoidant, self-deprecating, passive

Famous Pisces

Justin Bieber • Kurt Cobain • Glennon Doyle • Steve Jobs
Spike Lee • John Lewis • Catherine O'Hara • Rihanna
Nina Simone • Dr. Seuss

THE UNIVERSE IS YOURS

TO EXPAND

PISCES

PISCES

FOLLOW
YOUR
INTUITION

1-800-VIBE-WITH-ME

YOU
LIFT
ME
UP

WE ARE ALL MADE OF STARS

FIRE
& AIR

Fire Signs
Aries | Leo | Sagittarius

Blessed with the gift of fire, these signs of the Zodiac
bring out a person's enthusiasm and spontaneity. Fire
signs are typically energetic, inspiring, and independent.
They often have to keep their impulsivity in check.

Air Signs
Gemini | Libra | Aquarius

Air signs are thinkers, ponderers, and weighers of
options. Those born under Gemini, Libra, or Aquarius tend
to be pretty brainy and love the art of communication.
These folks must be kept on their toes, as they can fall
into restlessness easily.

WATER & EARTH

Water Signs
Cancer | Scorpio | Pisces

Just as waves can quickly transform from gentle and lapping to choppy and violent, so, too, can water signs. Water influences a person's emotional being; water signs can be moody, but they are also thoughtful, spiritual, and super in touch with their feelings.

Earth Signs
Taurus | Virgo | Capricorn

An earth sign can help you plant your feet firmly on the ground. Tauruses, Virgos, and Capricorns are considered stable and pragmatic, with a proclivity toward earthly delights—they can also be very sensual and loving.

DESTINED TO SHINE BRIGHT

HOT STUFF

WE ARE ALL CHILDREN OF MOTHER EARTH

BE THE FLOW

SUN CHILD

STAR CHILD

RIDE THE WAVE

BROADEN YOUR HORIZON

YOU ARE
MY SUN
MY MOON
AND ALL
MY STARS

SOUL SEEKER

I OPEN MYSELF TO GUIDANCE FROM THE UNIVERSE

BRB. Making my Saturn return.

PALM READING
CLUB

BRING
THE
SHADOWS
OF YOUR
MIND
TO LIGHT.

SPICY

LOL
IS MERCURY IN RETROGRADE

THE STARS INCLINE US
THEY DO NOT
BIND US

SUN, MOON, & RISING

If you know your birth date, place, and the exact time you were born, a quick search online will lead you to your star chart. At first blush, this circular diagram can be overwhelming, so let's break down the most important three signs in your chart:

SUN SIGN:

Your sun sign is your standard, determined-by-your-date-of-birth Zodiac sign. This sign represents the essence of who you are—your personality at its core, your identity, your ego.

MOON SIGN:

Your moon sign is a reflection of your emotional nature—how you process feelings, how you offer support to others, how you respond to your instincts and vulnerability.

RISING SIGN:

Your rising sign represents the planet that was on the eastern horizon at the time of your birth. It is often referred to as your social mask. Your sun sign may be in the fiery sign of Aries, but if your rising sign is the watery, sensitive Cancer, that might be the side of you others see first.

THE
PLANETS

The sun in the sky at the time of your birth has a huge impact on your identity. So does the moon. It's only natural that the rest of the planets in our solar system have some sort of gravitational pull on your personality, too. When you're able to dig deeper into your star chart, the astrological signs that align with each of the planets (except Earth . . . and yes, Pluto counts as a ruling planet in our mystical world) will illuminate different facets of your personality.

- Mercury: Communication, logic, intellect
- Venus: Love, passion, beauty
- Mars: Aggression, sexuality, action
- Jupiter: Luck, expansion, optimism
- Saturn: Responsibility, discipline, limits
- Uranus: Freedom, revolution, innovation
- Neptune: Spirituality, imagination, dreams
- Pluto: Power, transformation, control

SPRING EQUINOX

FALL EQUINOX

SUMMER SOLSTICE

WINTER SOLSTICE

ONE DAY AT A TIME + ONE DAY AT A TIME + ONE DAY AT A TIME

U · G C O ✴ T ✦ T C H ✳ I ✦ S

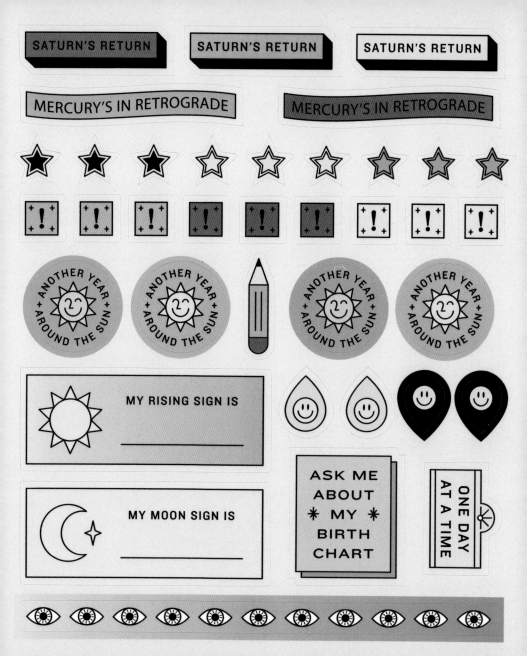

SATURN'S RETURN

SATURN'S RETURN

SATURN'S RETURN

MERCURY'S IN RETROGRADE

MERCURY'S IN RETROGRADE

ANOTHER YEAR · AROUND THE SUN ·

ANOTHER YEAR · AROUND THE SUN ·

ANOTHER YEAR · AROUND THE SUN ·

ANOTHER YEAR · AROUND THE SUN ·

MY RISING SIGN IS

_____

MY MOON SIGN IS

_____

ASK ME ABOUT * MY * BIRTH CHART

ONE DAY AT A TIME

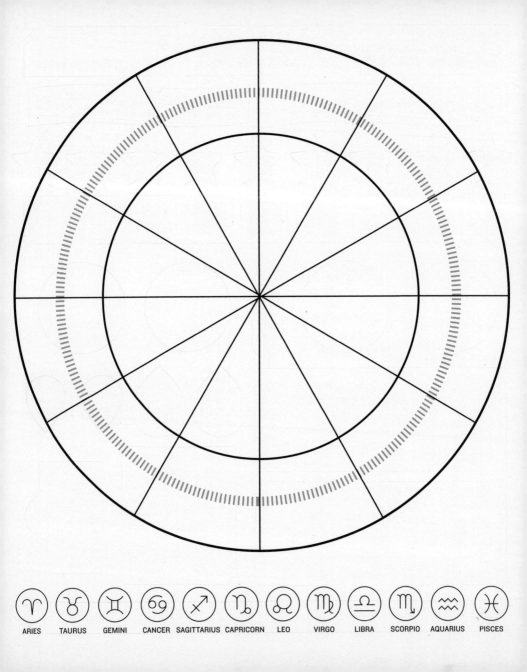

ARIES TAURUS GEMINI CANCER SAGITTARIUS CAPRICORN LEO VIRGO LIBRA SCORPIO AQUARIUS PISCES

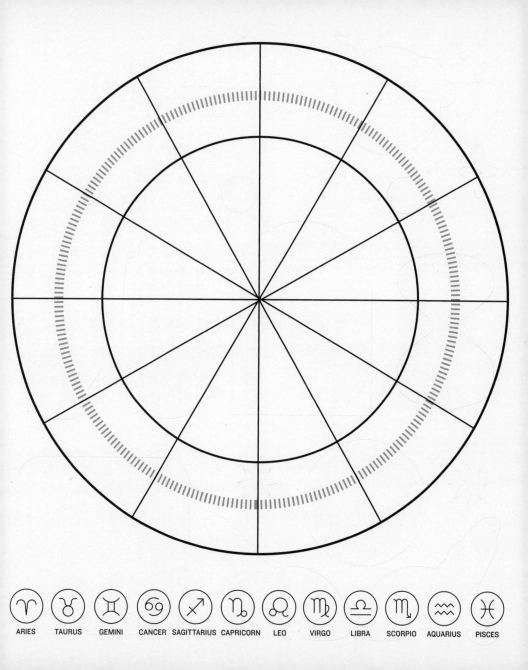

ARIES TAURUS GEMINI CANCER SAGITTARIUS CAPRICORN LEO VIRGO LIBRA SCORPIO AQUARIUS PISCES

EVERY DAY
IS A
BLESSING

WHAT GOES AROUND COMES AROUND

TAKE IT SLOW
IT'S
OK

HERE FOR A GOOD TIME NOT A LONG TIME

+ · HELLO · +
MY SIGN IS

FOUNTAIN
OF
YOUTH

LIVE
IN THE
NOW

BRB   BRB

CHANNELING
MY ENERGY

BE
LIGHT

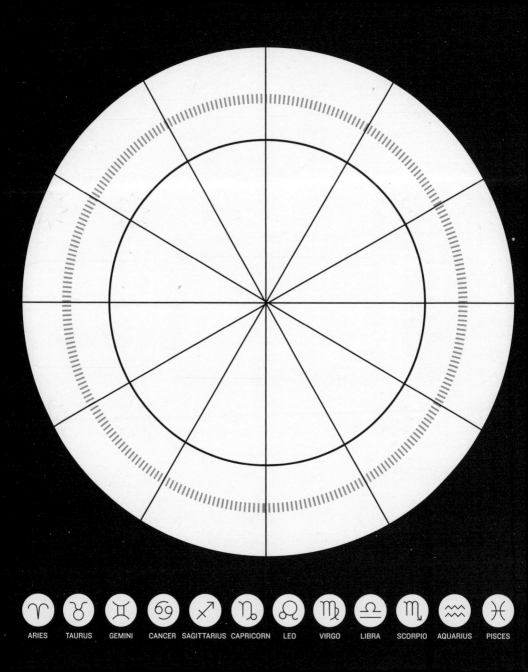

ARIES TAURUS GEMINI CANCER SAGITTARIUS CAPRICORN LEO VIRGO LIBRA SCORPIO AQUARIUS PISCES

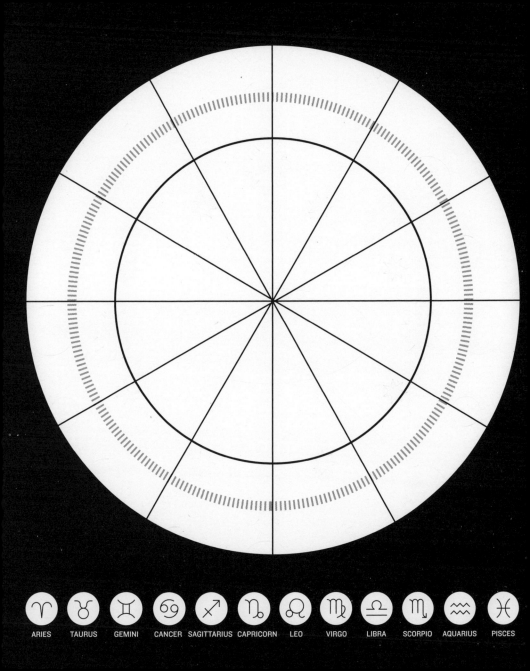

ARIES TAURUS GEMINI CANCER SAGITTARIUS CAPRICORN LEO VIRGO LIBRA SCORPIO AQUARIUS PISCES

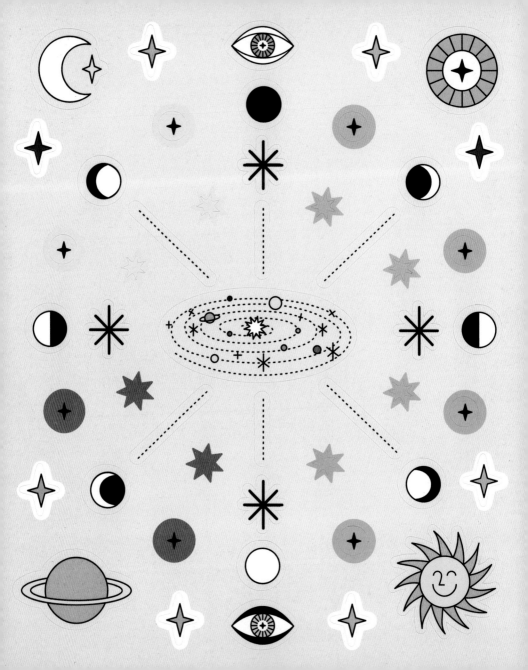

ARIES

ELEMENT:
Fire

MODALITY:
Cardinal

PLANETARY RULER:
Mars

ASTROLOGICAL OPPOSITE:
Libra

The Ram
March 21–April 19

AT THEIR BEST:
Courageous, enthusiastic, independent, bold, ambitious

AT THEIR WORST:
Willful, aggressive, selfish, impulsive, childlike

Famous Aries

Maya Angelou · Alec Baldwin · Ram Dass · Lady Gaga
Hugh Hefner · Elton John · Lil Nas X · Nancy Pelosi
Diana Ross · Reese Witherspoon

TAURUS

ELEMENT:
Earth

MODALITY:
Fixed

PLANETARY
RULER:
Venus

ASTROLOGICAL
OPPOSITE:
Scorpio

The Bull
April 20–May 20

AT THEIR BEST:
Dependable, patient,
resourceful, generous,
compassionate

AT THEIR WORST:
Rigid, vain, indulgent,
possessive, insecure

Famous Taurus

Aidy Bryant • John Cena • Cher • Tina Fey • Gigi Hadid
Janet Jackson • Dwayne "The Rock" Johnson
Grace Jones • Lizzo • Sam Smith

DO NOT FEAR CHANGE

YOU ARE
STRONGER
THAN
YOU THINK

TAURUS

TAURUS

TAURUS

EVOLVE

OR
REPEAT

MANIFESTING
CURRENT MOOD
MY DREAMS

trust
your
gut

GEMINI

ONE STEP AT A TIME

HERE 4 U

YOU LIGHT UP MY LIFE

Reminder
No feeling is final.

Repeat

Thank You!

LEAVE
HUMANITY
BETTER
THAN YOU
FOUND IT

GEMINI

WE ALL NEED REST
TO DO OUR BEST

GEMINI

ELEMENT:
Air

MODALITY:
Mutable

PLANETARY RULER:
Mercury

ASTROLOGICAL OPPOSITE:
Sagittarius

The Twins
May 21–June 20

AT THEIR BEST:
Communicative, curious, witty, charming, intelligent

AT THEIR WORST:
Restless, manipulative, nervous, unreliable, gossipy

Famous Gemini

Naomi Campbell • James Charles • Bob Dylan • Prince
John F. Kennedy • Kanye West • Marilyn Monroe
Kendrick Lamar • Stevie Nicks • Mary-Kate and Ashley Olsen

CANCER

ELEMENT:
Water

MODALITY:
Cardinal

PLANETARY RULER:
Moon

ASTROLOGICAL OPPOSITE:
Capricorn

The Crab
June 21–July 22

AT THEIR BEST:
Sensitive, nurturing, imaginative, perceptive, supportive

AT THEIR WORST:
Moody, suspicious, smothering, insecure, closed off

Famous Cancer

Anthony Bourdain • Larry David • Lana del Rey
Elizabeth Gilbert • Ariana Grande • Kevin Hart • Post Malone
Meryl Streep • Robin Williams • Malala Yousafzai

LEO

ELEMENT:
Fire

MODALITY:
Fixed

**PLANETARY
RULER:**
Sun

**ASTROLOGICAL
OPPOSITE:**
Aquarius

The Lion
July 23–August 22

AT THEIR BEST:
Creative, enthusiastic,
playful, funny, affectionate

AT THEIR WORST:
Dramatic, codependent,
arrogant, self-absorbed,
domineering

Famous Leo

James Baldwin • Coolio • Mick Jagger • Kylie Jenner

Dan Levy • Jennifer Lopez • Madonna • Barack Obama

Maya Rudolph • Martha Stewart

VIRGO

ELEMENT:
Earth

MODALITY:
Mutable

PLANETARY RULER:
Mercury

ASTROLOGICAL OPPOSITE:
Pisces

The Maiden
August 23–September 22

AT THEIR BEST:
Thoughtful, hardworking, loyal, sensitive, practical

AT THEIR WORST:
Rigid, worrying, judgmental, overly critical, righteous

Famous Virgo

Chimamanda Ngozi Adichie · Beyoncé · Leonard Cohen
Blake Lively · Freddie Mercury · Bill Murray · Mother Teresa
Bernie Sanders · Amy Winehouse · Zendaya

MIND   PROGRESS   CHANGE

LET'S GROW TOGETHER

VIRGO

TRUST + THE + PROCESS

IT'S OK YOU'RE ONLY HUMAN

THINGS I OVER-THOUGHT

VOL 10

VIRGO

You Got This

LIBRA

ELEMENT:
Air

MODALITY:
Cardinal

PLANETARY RULER:
Venus

ASTROLOGICAL OPPOSITE:
Aries

The Scales
September 23–October 22

AT THEIR BEST:
Intellectual, charming, romantic, balanced, adaptable

AT THEIR WORST:
Dishonest, indecisive, avoidant, people-pleasing, neurotic

Famous Libra

Cardi B • Ta-Nehisi Coates • Snoop Dogg • Kamala Harris
Kim Kardashian West • Marie Kondo • Gwyneth Paltrow
Alexandria Ocasio-Cortez • Bruce Springsteen • Serena Williams

SCORPIO

ELEMENT:
Water

MODALITY:
Fixed

PLANETARY RULER:
Mars

ASTROLOGICAL OPPOSITE:
Taurus

The Scorpion
October 23–November 21

AT THEIR BEST:
Intense, mysterious, intuitive, passionate, investigative

AT THEIR WORST:
Explosive, vengeful, obsessive, possessive, destructive

Famous Scorpio

Joe Biden • Björk • Drake • Bill Gates • Joni Mitchell
Frank Ocean • Pablo Picasso • Sylvia Plath
Tracee Ellis Ross • Winona Ryder

FOLLOW
* YOUR *
INTUITION

Scorpio

SCORPIO

IT'S OKAY TO BE VULNERABLE

FOLLOW YOUR ENERGY
FOLLOW YOUR ENERGY

TRUST
YOUR
GUT

ENJOY YOUR TIME ALIVE

SAGITTARIUS

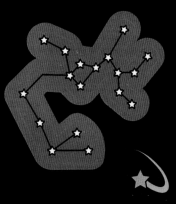

LIFE IS AN ADVENTURE

SAGITTARIUS

FREE SPIRIT

SHINE BRIGHT

WHERE YOUR FOCUS GOES YOUR ENERGY SHALL FLOW

SAGITTARIUS

ELEMENT:
Fire

MODALITY:
Mutable

PLANETARY RULER:
Jupiter

ASTROLOGICAL OPPOSITE:
Gemini

The Archer
November 22–December 21

AT THEIR BEST:
Adventurous, spontaneous, idealistic, wise, honest

AT THEIR WORST:
Impatient, fanatic, restless, confrontational, frank

Famous Sagittarius

Shirley Chisholm • Walt Disney • Billie Eilish • Jay-Z
Nicki Minaj • Jim Morrison • Brad Pitt • Britney Spears
Taylor Swift • Chrissy Teigen

CAPRICORN

ELEMENT:
Earth

MODALITY:
Cardinal

PLANETARY
RULER:
Saturn

ASTROLOGICAL
OPPOSITE:
Cancer

The Sea Goat
December 22–January 19

AT THEIR BEST:
Ambitious, grounded,
distinguished, disciplined,
dependable

AT THEIR WORST:
Materialistic, stubborn,
controlling, opportunistic,
overly guarded

Famous Capricorn

David Bowie · Timothée Chalamet · Janis Joplin
Martin Luther King Jr. · Richard Nixon · Lin-Manuel Miranda
Michelle Obama · Dolly Parton · Shonda Rhimes · Patti Smith

NO TIME FOR BAD ENERGY

12
9 3
6

PROTECT YOUR PEACE

CAP RI CORN →

CAPRICORN

RELAX YOUR MIND

DAILY MANTRA
I CAN ACHIEVE
ANYTHING
I SET
MY MIND TO

BE THE CHANGE YOU WISH TO SEE

EYE ON THE PRIZE

AQUARIUS

VISIONARY

AQUARIUS

AQUARIUS

ELEMENT:
Air

MODALITY:
Fixed

PLANETARY
RULER:
Saturn

ASTROLOGICAL
OPPOSITE:
Leo

The Water Bearer
January 20–February 18

AT THEIR BEST:
Rebellious, insightful,
self-assured, original,
progressive

AT THEIR WORST:
Aloof, unpredictable,
stubborn, shocking,
detached

Famous Aquarius

Angela Davis • James Dean • Ellen DeGeneres
Guy Fieri • Toni Morrison • Yoko Ono • Ed Sheeran
Megan Thee Stallion • Harry Styles • Oprah Winfrey

PISCES

ELEMENT:
Water

MODALITY:
Mutable

**PLANETARY
RULER:**
Jupiter

**ASTROLOGICAL
OPPOSITE:**
Virgo

The Fish
February 19–March 20

AT THEIR BEST:
Intuitive, creative, sensitive,
compassionate, spiritual

AT THEIR WORST:
Self-indulgent, spacey,
avoidant, self-deprecating,
passive

Famous Pisces

Justin Bieber • Kurt Cobain • Glennon Doyle • Steve Jobs
Spike Lee • John Lewis • Catherine O'Hara • Rihanna
Nina Simone • Dr. Seuss

THE UNIVERSE IS YOURS

TO EXPAND

PISCES

PISCES

FOLLOW
YOUR
INTUITION

I-800-VIBE-WITH-ME

YOU
LIFT
ME
UP

WE ARE ALL
MADE
OF
STARS

FIRE & AIR

Fire Signs
Aries | Leo | Sagittarius

Blessed with the gift of fire, these signs of the Zodiac
bring out a person's enthusiasm and spontaneity. Fire
signs are typically energetic, inspiring, and independent.
They often have to keep their impulsivity in check.

Air Signs
Gemini | Libra | Aquarius

Air signs are thinkers, ponderers, and weighers of
options. Those born under Gemini, Libra, or Aquarius tend
to be pretty brainy and love the art of communication.
These folks must be kept on their toes, as they can fall
into restlessness easily.

WATER & EARTH

Water Signs
Cancer | Scorpio | Pisces

Just as waves can quickly transform from gentle and lapping to choppy and violent, so, too, can water signs. Water influences a person's emotional being; water signs can be moody, but they are also thoughtful, spiritual, and super in touch with their feelings.

Earth Signs
Taurus | Virgo | Capricorn

An earth sign can help you plant your feet firmly on the ground. Tauruses, Virgos, and Capricorns are considered stable and pragmatic, with a proclivity toward earthly delights—they can also be very sensual and loving.

DESTINED TO SHINE BRIGHT

HOT STUFF

WE ARE ALL CHILDREN OF MOTHER EARTH

BE THE FLOW

SUN CHILD

STAR CHILD

RIDE THE WAVE

BROADEN YOUR HORIZON

SUN, MOON, & RISING

If you know your birth date, place, and the exact time you were born, a quick search online will lead you to your star chart. At first blush, this circular diagram can be overwhelming, so let's break down the most important three signs in your chart:

SUN SIGN:

Your sun sign is your standard, determined-by-your-date-of-birth Zodiac sign. This sign represents the essence of who you are—your personality at its core, your identity, your ego.

MOON SIGN:

Your moon sign is a reflection of your emotional nature—how you process feelings, how you offer support to others, how you respond to your instincts and vulnerability.

RISING SIGN:

Your rising sign represents the planet that was on the eastern horizon at the time of your birth. It is often referred to as your social mask. Your sun sign may be in the fiery sign of Aries, but if your rising sign is the watery, sensitive Cancer, that might be the side of you others see first.

THE PLANETS

The sun in the sky at the time of your birth has a huge impact on your identity. So does the moon. It's only natural that the rest of the planets in our solar system have some sort of gravitational pull on your personality, too. When you're able to dig deeper into your star chart, the astrological signs that align with each of the planets (except Earth . . . and yes, Pluto counts as a ruling planet in our mystical world) will illuminate different facets of your personality.

- Mercury: Communication, logic, intellect
- Venus: Love, passion, beauty
- Mars: Aggression, sexuality, action
- Jupiter: Luck, expansion, optimism
- Saturn: Responsibility, discipline, limits
- Uranus: Freedom, revolution, innovation
- Neptune: Spirituality, imagination, dreams
- Pluto: Power, transformation, control

SPRING EQUINOX

FALL EQUINOX

SUMMER SOLSTICE

WINTER SOLSTICE

ONE DAY AT A TIME + ONE DAY AT A TIME + ONE DAY AT A TIME

U G C O T T C H I S

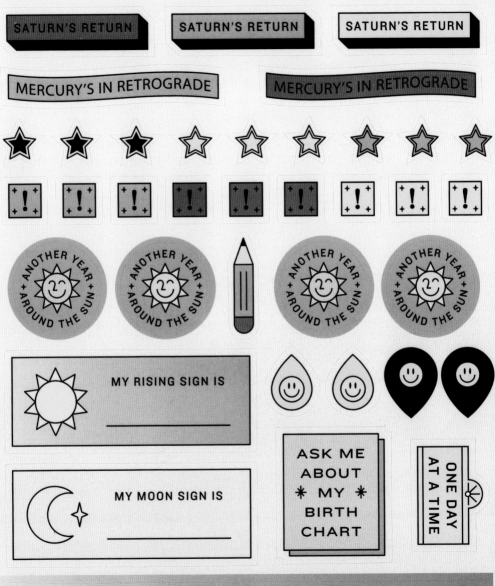

SATURN'S RETURN
SATURN'S RETURN
SATURN'S RETURN

MERCURY'S IN RETROGRADE
MERCURY'S IN RETROGRADE

ANOTHER YEAR + AROUND THE SUN
ANOTHER YEAR + AROUND THE SUN
ANOTHER YEAR + AROUND THE SUN
ANOTHER YEAR + AROUND THE SUN

MY RISING SIGN IS
_____

MY MOON SIGN IS
_____

ASK ME ABOUT * MY * BIRTH CHART

ONE DAY AT A TIME

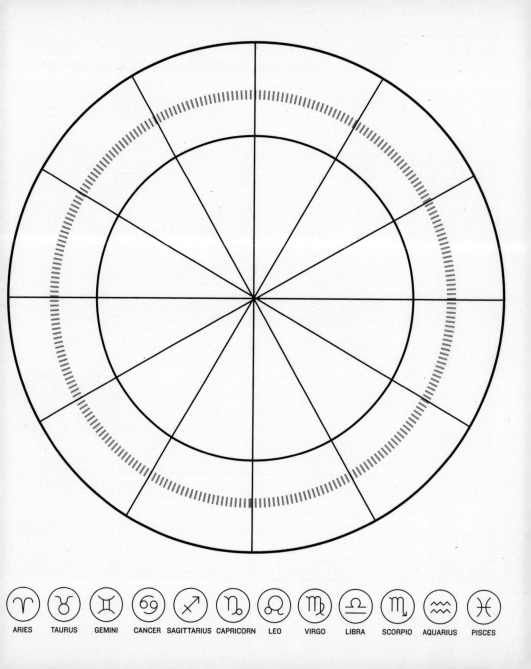

ARIES   TAURUS   GEMINI   CANCER   SAGITTARIUS   CAPRICORN   LEO   VIRGO   LIBRA   SCORPIO   AQUARIUS   PISCES

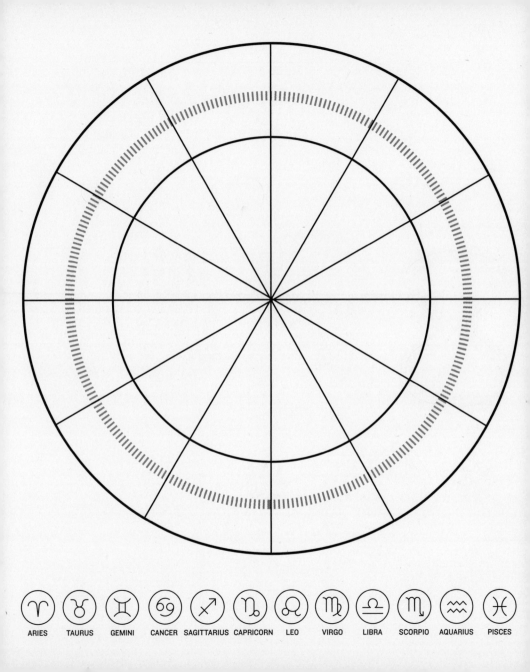

ARIES   TAURUS   GEMINI   CANCER SAGITTARIUS CAPRICORN   LEO   VIRGO   LIBRA   SCORPIO AQUARIUS   PISCES

EVERY DAY
IS A
BLESSING

WHAT GOES AROUND COMES AROUND

TAKE IT SLOW
IT'S
OK

HERE FOR
A
GOOD TIME
NOT
A
LONG TIME

· · **HELLO** · ·
MY SIGN IS

FOUNTAIN
OF
YOUTH

LIVE
IN THE
NOW

BRB   BRB

CHANNELING
MY ENERGY

BE
LIGHT

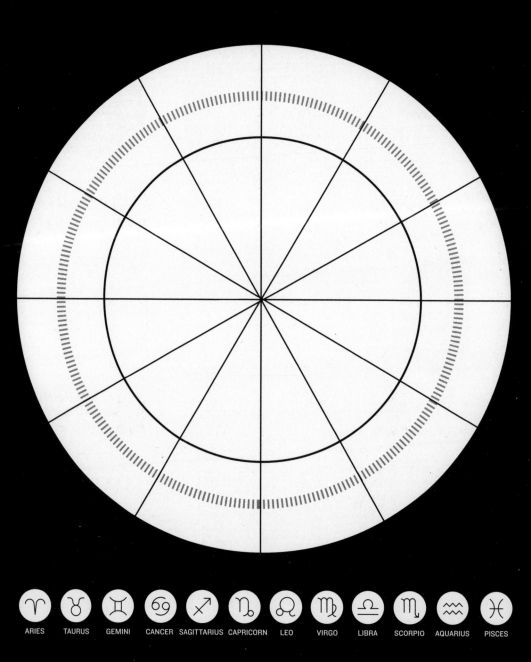

ARIES TAURUS GEMINI CANCER SAGITTARIUS CAPRICORN LEO VIRGO LIBRA SCORPIO AQUARIUS PISCES

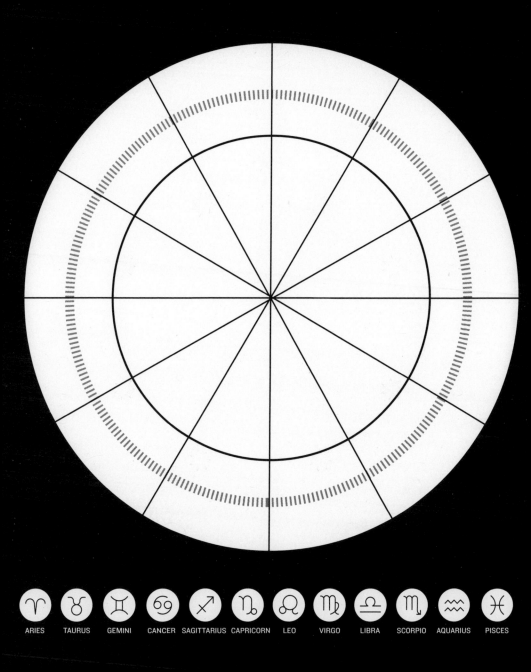

ARIES TAURUS GEMINI CANCER SAGITTARIUS CAPRICORN LEO VIRGO LIBRA SCORPIO AQUARIUS PISCES

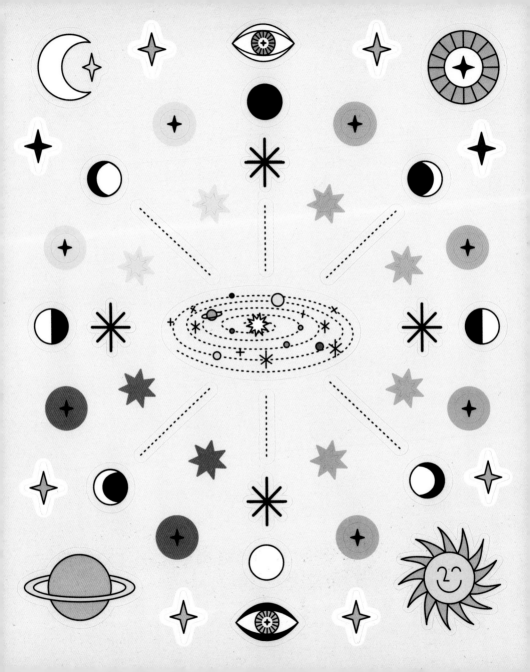